The Strange Beast

Explorer Challenge

Find out what
the bird eats ...

OXFORD
UNIVERSITY PRESS

The children were playing a game.
"I'm thinking of an animal," said Wilma.

"Has it got four legs?" asked Chip.
"Yes," said Wilma.

They did not ask more questions as the key began to glow.

"I hope it will take us to a place
with lots of animals!" said Biff.

The magic took them back in time to a castle. A crowd was waiting outside the castle gates.

Why are we *here?*

7

"We are waiting to see a strange beast!"
a boy said eagerly.

"It is coming from a land far away," added a woman. "It will live in the king's zoo."

9

Suddenly they heard people shouting.
The people sounded frightened.
"The beast is coming!" cried the boy.

"People say the beast is bigger and stronger than twenty adults!" said a woman.
"But what *is* the beast?" asked Biff.

"Look," said Wilf. "It's an *elephant*! These people have never seen one before."

The people in the crowd were
not excited now.
They were afraid.

"The beast is as big as a house!" shouted a man.
"It will eat us all!"
"Elephants eat plants, not people!" said Chip.

The elephant did not like all the noise.
It reared up on to its back legs.

"It is angry!" shouted a woman. "It
will trample us!"

"It is *not* angry," said Wilma. "It is frightened."
She grabbed two apples from a cart.

Wilma held out one apple.
Carefully the elephant took it with its
long trunk.

The people in the crowd began to smile.
They loved the strange beast now!

The key was glowing. It was time to go home.

"We didn't finish our game," said Chip. "Has your animal got a long nose?"
"Yes!" said Wilma.

Retell the Story

Look at the pictures and retell the story in your own words.

Look Back, Explorers

Where was the elephant going to live?

What did the man say the elephant was as big as?

Why did the people change their minds about the 'strange beast'?

Imagine talking to someone who has never seen an elephant. How would you describe an elephant to them?

Did you find out what the bird ate?

What's Next, Explorers?

Now you have read about Wilma feeding the elephant, find out about what lots of other animals eat ...

Beast Feasts

Anita Ganeri
Series created by Roderick Hunt and Alex Brychta

OXFORD

Explorer Challenge
for *Beast Feasts*

Find out whose tongue
this is ...